OWLS

First published in Great Britain in 1997 by
Colin Baxter Photography Ltd.,
Grantown-on-Spey,
Moray PH26 3NA
Scotland

Reprinted 2000

A CIP Catalogue record for this book is available from the British Library

ISBN 1-900455-23-4

Photographs © 1997:

Printed in China

OWLS

Keith Graham

Colin Baxter Photography, Grantown-on-Spey, Scotland

Introduction

Owls are wise, sagacious, learned and even professorial. At least, that is the impression most people have of these curiously humanoid birds. The pronounced facial disc, the large, front-facing eyes, a hooked beak rather resembling a hooked nose and, in the case of the long-eared and short-eared varieties, the 'ears', which are not ears at all but feathered tufts, amplify this perception of owls. To accentuate the impression, owls also have stocky, square bodies.

To confirm this anthropomorphic view, most of us were weaned on children's stories which cast the owl in the role of the wise old sage, the academic of the avian world. Hence there are countless representations of owls manifested in clay, porcelain, pottery, metal and wooden ornaments, not to mention as many versions in the realm of soft toys. In this respect, perhaps, they vie only with penguins as inert decorations or playthings because they are vertically orientated birds with human characteristics, to which the human presumably warms as a kindred spirit.

Yet owls are killers. Their whole lifestyle as deadly predators depends upon their ability to seek out food and despatch it. Using a range of weaponry which long predates man's sophisticated technology, such as a radar-like ability to home in on potential victims in total darkness, almost silent flight and a lethal pair of talons, the final *coup de grâce* is achieved with that sharp curved beak which, in many people's eyes, represents a nose. Perhaps this aspect of the owl's character is not recognised beneath its disguise of relatively billowing plumage and its apparently human features, or not understood by those whose contact with owls is either through a plethora of ornaments and soft toys, or, as is mostly the case, as a result of audible rather than visual acquaintance. This is perhaps especially so with Britain's most commonplace owl, the tawny or 'brown' owl, with which a relatively large percentage of us are familiar, simply because it is a resident of both town and country.

Tawny owl at its daytime roost. This is a 'grey-phase' bird.

Yet seldom do even tawny owls reveal themselves to anyone but the most observant. Their lifestyle is, by any stretch of the imagination, nocturnal and thus covert and it is probably their hooting and shrieking with which people are most familiar. Unlike ideal children, owls are usually heard but not seen.

There is of course, another perception of owls which is less heart-warming. Those hootings and shriekings of tawny owls, the screeching and hissing of barn owls and, on occasion, the moaning hoots of long-eared owls, have been known almost to petrify people in whom ignorance of the source of such ethereal sounds, and the almost total absence of visual contact, has evoked terror and fear. Equally, the ghostly flitting of barn owls in the gloaming has also given rise to suspicion and fear, and, particularly in less enlightened times, not least to associations with the spirit world.

Fear of owls is not necessarily confined to our more superstitious ancestors. Even today there are those who exhibit what can only be described as an in-built aversion to them, especially at close quarters. Some years ago, I reared a tawny owl chick which had fallen from its nest to be duly rescued by a well-meaning family who, finding the task of rearing the foundling messy and difficult, consigned it to my care. It was to be the first of many such foundlings to pass through my hands.

The creature – no more than a bundle of greyish white down, to which were attached two large feet equipped with exceptionally sharp talons and an equally sharp beak which it constantly clicked when approached – rejoiced in the name 'Mohammed Owly'! Once accustomed to the daily routine of being fed, the early aggression abated and within a week the bird was happy to perch on my wrist. When a friend visited, who was an articulate university lecturer, I was moved to introduce him to the owlet, only to find that when I entered the room with the bird quietly perched upon my wrist, the said lecturer retreated to the furthest corner of the room and beseeched me not to bring the bird any closer. For reasons he was unable to explain, this normally phlegmatic individual was terrified of the bird!

Graveyards provide habitat for mice and voles – hence the presence of the 'ghostly' barn owl.

*Little owls nest in holes in trees, as well as cracks and crevices in walls,
using no additional materials to line the natural cavity.*

Many cultures, of course, have been wary or fearful of owls. Several factors in owl behaviour combined to cast it in the role of a precursor of doom. The hooting and screeching of an owl was believed by the Romans to foretell an imminent death. The fact that owls, notably barn and tawny owls, often occupy the ruins of buildings, seemingly added credence to the supposition that owls were, in essence, bad news. Even biblical references are not on their side. They are variously described as 'unclean', certainly never to be eaten and as 'abominations'.

On the other hand, Arab folklore casts owls in the role of the spirits of those who were unavenged at their deaths. Here in Britain, as elsewhere in Europe, it was at one time a custom to nail the remains of a slaughtered owl to the door of a barn as a deterrent to other evil spirits.

Conversely, down the centuries, generations of farmers have been only too happy to see owls, presumably mostly barn or tawny owls, taking up residence in their buildings. The prowess of these two species as slayers of 'vermin', mainly rats and mice, which caused havoc in grain stores, made them very much the farmers' friends. Indeed, historically, the design of farm buildings always took into account the residential needs of owls. Spaces were made to accommodate them and only since the dawn of the steel structured, sheeting-clad buildings of modern farm construction, has this rule been forgotten. Purpose-built, prefabricated farm buildings have denied barn owls suitable nesting sites. In recent years, to emphasise this point further, conservationists have gone to considerable lengths to introduce artificial nesting boxes to many of these modern structures with variable degrees of success.

There are four native owls in Britain, the most numerous being the tawny owl, an inhabitant of woodland which has also successfully invaded the man-made environment of town and city parks and gardens. The quite startlingly beautiful barn owl was once widespread throughout lowland rural areas of Britain but has been in decline for several decades. The short-eared owl is nomadic in lifestyle, inhabiting open moorlands and young forestry plantations, whereas the long-eared owl is very much a denizen of woodland.

To these four species may be added the little owl, which was introduced to southern

Britain from Continental Europe in the nineteenth century and has since colonised much of England and Wales. It is now established also in southern Scotland, albeit in small numbers thus far. Another addition is the snowy owl, which is a polar bird but has been known to visit northern parts of Scotland during the past two centuries. Breeding was recorded in Shetland during the 1960s and 1970s and since then, individual birds have been seen, but permanence as a breeding species has not been established. From time to time other owls have been recorded, mostly as vagrants from elsewhere in Europe.

Barn Owl

Of all the owls, the barn owl is surely the most attractive. From a distance its plumage is buff on the upper parts and white beneath. Closer inspection reveals an intricately patterned plumage in which the buff colouration takes on a golden hue. The flecked but subtle black, grey and white also translate to silver to give this bird the most fantastic, regal appearance. The Continental race is perceptibly darker, in some cases almost entirely lacking the white frontage on the breast.

In Britain, the paler race is often perceived as a ghostly figure floating through trees, along roadsides and hedgerows, or over pastures and rough, uncultivated land, its buoyant flight often undulating, eyes trained on the ground below. Frequently the bird will pirouette before stooping, plunging feet first into the vegetation to seize its prey, wings held aloft. The white facial disc accentuates the impression of a large, blunt head, so characteristic of all owls.

Dusk and dawn are almost always the best times to see barn owls in action during the breeding season, but they may also sometimes be seen hunting in broad daylight, especially when they have young to feed. Nature has equipped owls with its own brand of technology. The barn owl's eyes are not quite as large and prominent as those of other British owls, but there can be no doubt that, even in the poorest light, it can see extremely well.

Hearing may also play an important role in the successful completion of a hunting

Barn owls favour lowland farmland and are most commonly seen at dusk or dawn.

The buoyant, measured flight of a barn owl as it carefully quarters its hunting territory. Dark eyes focus intently on the ground as it seeks out the slightest movement that might betray the presence of a mouse or vole. Slightly offset ears also enable this well-honed predator to detect its prey, radar-like, by sound alone.

sortie. In fact the ears, hidden beneath the plumage behind the facial disc, are large and slightly offset, one marginally higher than the other. Thus, in virtually complete darkness, a barn owl is still able to pinpoint its prey. For example, the rustling progress of a mouse across the floor of a barn is quickly heard, and by tilting its head the owl can locate precisely the source of the rustling and then launch itself unerringly towards the target as if guided by radar.

Furthermore, the attack is launched on virtually silent wings. The soft fringes of the main flight feathers eliminate sound and before the mouse knows what has hit it, it is dead, seized in the deadly talons which, in owls, unlike most other raptors, have two toes forward and two back.

Prey is generally swallowed whole, except when the food is being taken for the youngsters in the first few weeks of their lives. Then, the hooked beak, rather longer and narrower than that of other owls, is used to dissect or tear the creature into bits.

As is the case with all raptors, barn owls disgorge the unwanted parts of their prey in the form of pellets which contain bones, fur and, where small birds also feature on the menu, feathers. Barn owl pellets, usually discarded at regular roosting places and nesting sites, are noticeably black and shiny. Roughage of this kind is apparently essential to the digestive system and analysis of pellets is the easiest way of discovering exactly what the birds are eating.

Barn owls don't always nest in rural buildings. Caves, cliffs and tree cavities are also used. The nest itself is unembellished with building materials and, more often than not, the eggs are laid on a mattress of pellets. The eggs are white and the number laid will reflect the availability of food, perhaps only three or four in a lean year, but up to ten in a year of plenty. Incubation is the prerogative of the hen bird although the cock is seldom far away and for long hours will roost beside his brooding mate.

Incubation lasts for just over a month and laying can take place between April and June. The youngsters are covered with short white down, comical sights as they grow, with spindly legs which are longer than those of other owls and 'slitty' eyes. As the down is gradually replaced by feathers – the wing feathers are the first to appear – they look even more comical. A further curious characteristic is the continual hissing which emanates from them, especially when the parents arrive with food. It is generally some ten weeks before the youngsters fledge and leave the nest.

As with all other owls, the eggs hatch at relatively long intervals so that a single brood can reveal considerable disparity in that the first hatched chick may have virtually full juvenile plumage, while the last may still be almost entirely covered in down. In particularly good years, a second brood may follow later in the summer.

Although barn owls may be regarded largely as rurally based birds, this is not always the case. A year or two ago, a pair set up home in the chimney stack of a large town house which had been divided into flats. Their home was thus situated high above the busy main street of one of Scotland's most popular tourist towns, through which pass a substantial number of heavy vehicles – hardly a peaceful, rural setting. The adults appeared to obtain most of their food from the fields on the edge of the town, or from the edges of the woodlands which rise steeply above it.

Their presence caused some concern among pedestrians who, if they were walking on the same side of the road as the building, could only hear the hissings, snoring and shriekings but could neither see nor identify the source of the noises. Several were accordingly sent hurrying on their way in some consternation!

It has already been established that the barn owl, in particular, has for long been regarded as the farmers' ally, a destroyer of farmyard pests. How ironic therefore, that as farming technology has advanced, especially during the latter part of the twentieth century, the barn owl has become an unwitting victim of these developments, its numbers decimated in many parts of the country.

The decline has been more marked in the most intensively farmed areas. It seems certain that the substantial increase in the use of chemicals, most notably of organo-chlorine pesticides, has had a seriously deleterious effect upon barn owls. These chemicals pass quickly through the food chain. Mice and voles which consume treated seeds are, in turn,

The barn owl's gold and silver upper plumage contrasts sharply with its white face and breast.

A perfect landing. Fine fringing on the main flight feathers deaden wing sound and add to the 'ghostly' image of this beautiful bird.

consumed by the owls – they are the primary source of food – and it follows that these toxic materials build up in the owls, affecting their ability to breed and ultimately causing death.

But that seems to be only part of the story. The most favoured hunting grounds for barn owls are of rough pasture and meadow, together with uncultivated land where rodents are plentiful. In the drive to exploit almost every available acre of land, for economic reasons, many such areas have been 'improved' and turned into productive agricultural land. Furthermore, many miles of hedgerow have also been stripped from the rural landscape of Britain. Such hedgerows are the perfect habitat for the rodents upon which the owls rely.

However, the expansion of forestry has been of benefit to barn owls. Young plantations, from which grazing animals are excluded, provide, in their first few years, excellent habitat for small rodents, notably short-tailed field voles. These rodent riches begin to diminish rapidly, however, once the trees approach maturity, exclude sunlight and, in time, extinguish the ground vegetation which shelters the rodents. Then it is time for the owls to move on. Roadside verges similarly provide good habitats for these small rodents, particularly for voles, and it is quite a familiar sight to see barn owls patrolling roadsides with their characteristically low, bobbing flight. Unfortunately, as a result, they become vulnerable to the traffic and are frequently catalogued as road casualties.

In recent times a more enlightened attitude towards conservation, together with fewer economic pressures, have resulted in a slow-down in the rate of land improvements. This, in addition to the increasing acreage of 'set-aside' land, has given the barn owl something of a lifeline in some parts of the country.

Although the barn owl is widely distributed across the globe, its decline has been most marked in Europe. Particularly hard winters undoubtedly contribute to short-term declines in population and, recognising that owl numbers in general inevitably fluctuate in direct correlation to variations in rodent numbers, the rapid advance of farming technology throughout Europe has clearly played a major role in their overall decline. In addition, improved storage of grain and the use of rodent poisons have depleted the number of mice and rats present in farmyards, while the poisons have entered the food chain.

Tawny Owls

Much more familiar to townsfolk are the weird hootings and 'kee-wicking' of tawny owls. It is generally thought that the hooting, familiarly translated as 'too-whit-to-whoo' but sometimes truncated to 'too-whit' or even a single 'whoo-whoo', is the call of the male with the shrill response, 'kee-wick', the call of the female. In late summer and autumn when territories are being established, there is much contact calling. If the barn owl has found changes to the modern world hard to cope with, the same cannot be said of the tawny or 'brown' owl. Although in essence a bird of woodland, the tawny has much more readily come to terms with the man-made environment and has consequently become commonplace in town and city parks and gardens.

The mottled plumage of the tawny conceals it most effectively, especially in its native woodland haunts. It, too, flies silently, equipped as it is with the same feather-fringing, and its sudden soundless appearance as it flaps across a city street and is illuminated by the street lights can be startling, to those of a nervous disposition.

There are two distinct colour variations, known as phases, of tawny owl present in Britain, brown and grey. In general, the birds of the grey phase give the appearance of being a little lighter in colour and this is most marked on and around the facial disc. Continental tawnies are inclined to be greyer and it is possible that the greyer British tawnies might, somewhere in their genes, have a trace of Continental ancestry. There appears to be no discrimination between birds of these two phases, with grey-phase and brown-phase owls quite happily pairing and breeding together.

When perched, the tawny owl presents the archetypal image we have of owls. Its large, round head, prominent facial disc with two large, front-facing eyes and that inevitably hooked 'nose', surmounting a square-shouldered, plump-looking body, seems to be a babyish, even cuddly figure. There are occasions, however, when a tawny will 'slim down', altering its shape by pressing its voluminous plumage close to its body and narrowing its eyes to diagonal slits. This happens when the bird is trying to make itself as

A tawny owl snatching a daytime rest. Tawnies are notoriously more active by night.

unobtrusive as possible, usually when other small birds are threatening or 'mobbing' it or when some unwitting human has invaded its territory. It will also often position itself close to the main trunk of the tree in which it is perched, again to merge more easily with its background.

The wings of the tawny owl are relatively short and often it progresses with quite rapid wingbeats, especially when flying over open ground. In less exposed situations, short, sharp wingbeats are interspersed with gentle glides. Short wings enable the owl to negotiate its passage through woodland with greater facility.

If its physical characteristics are often seen to make it resemble man, in practice they provide the owl with many advantages. Front-facing eyes with binocular vision enhance the bird's ability to focus accurately upon prey and gauge distance precisely. The eyes, of course, are huge in relation to our own. If we were to be equipped with eyes proportionately the same size as those of a tawny owl, and relative to the dimensions of our skull, they would be as large as tennis balls. Such enormous eyes are capable of gathering light very efficiently: in short, they can see in what we might regard as almost total darkness. If that were not enough, the tawny's hearing is also remarkably keen. As in the case of the barn owl, the ears are slightly offset, which allows the bird to pinpoint its prey precisely by sound, even if it cannot see it.

Rodents – shrews, mice, voles and rats – are of prime importance. Small birds also feature in the diet, and it may be assumed that the town and city residents exploit this resource very effectively, picking off roosting birds such as sparrows under the cover of darkness.

I once cared for a tawny owl which had become entangled in fishing line which was caught in trees by the side of a river and subsequently abandoned by the angler. Unfortunately, it was some days before the bird was discovered and by the time I managed to recover it, the main part of one wing had atrophied. Clearly the bird's struggles to free itself had served only to tighten the line round the wing and the blood supply had been cut off.

This tawny youngster of a few weeks, still clothed in down, has already left the nest.

The wing duly fell off and I was faced with having to look after a one-winged bird. This particular owl did not take kindly to captivity and no matter how I confined it, it somehow always managed to escape. For several years it lived in my orchard. Each day I fed it but it became increasingly obvious that it was supplementing the food I was giving it by picking off roosting birds at night. The pellets I recovered on occasions contained the recognisable remains of chaffinches and sometimes of voles too. Inevitably named 'Houdini', the bird had clearly adapted itself despite such a debilitating handicap and had learned to sidle along the branches under cover of darkness to snatch the small birds, and had also developed a technique of dropping on unsuspecting voles from a low perch.

The food provided by me was collected from ground level and it was amazing to see the bird descend through the branches, pick up its food and then clamber aloft again. The forward-facing eyes, like our own, enable owls to focus precisely on prey but, in addition, nature has given owls the ability to turn their heads through almost 360 degrees.

Tawny owls are doughty protectors of their young and dangerous adversaries. The well-known bird photographer, Eric Hosking, lost an eye when investigating a tawny owl nest. Those razor-sharp talons are capable of inflicting very painful damage! I have always taken the precaution of wearing a broad-brimmed hat when called upon to rescue a 'lost' tawny owl chick, or return one to its nest.

Traditionally, tawnies favour tree holes as nesting sites, sometimes a very deep fork in a tree. They take to nesting boxes readily and, like their barn owl cousins, do not trouble themselves with the business of nest building. Occasionally they will take over a crow's old nest or squirrel drey but actual nest construction is not for them. They also sometimes choose to nest in derelict buildings and just occasionally on cliff ledges. They have been known to nest on the ground, but rarely.

Territories are often formed in the autumn, hence the persistent vocalisation from late summer onwards; mating can sometimes occur as early as February. Most, however, content themselves with beginning their breeding season in late March or early April, the

A brown-phase tawny – ready for a night's hunting.

female usually producing three or four white and very spherical eggs, brooding them herself and incubating for about 29 days. Tawnies leave the nest at about 35 days and the vicinity of a tawny home is soon echoing to the constant wheezy calls of the youngsters as they continually demand food from their parents.

As is the case with all owls, tawnies have good and bad years according to the success or otherwise of the small mammals. The turnover in the breeding cycle of rodents is rapid indeed – a vole is sexually mature at six weeks of age. However, dry summers sometimes produce poorer breeding rates, which puts pressure on the tawny owl population. Owls will sometimes take worms and beetles as emergency rations in such circumstances.

In bad rodent years, the mortality among first-year tawny owls can be devastating. Sometimes more than 70% of the chicks produced in a year will not survive to see the following spring. In my experience, one frequent indication of a bad year reveals itself in the autumn and winter months when tawnies are frequently to be seen dining off the remains of road victim rabbits. It is, sadly, too often the case that these inexperienced birds perish the same way themselves, utterly dazzled and blinded by the lights of oncoming traffic.

Short-eared Owl

Unlike the dark eyes of barn and tawny owls, the short-eared owl has golden or yellow irises surrounding the black pupils, which give this ground-nesting member of the owl clan a truly baleful expression.

The short-eared owl is an inhabitant of open moorland and immature forestry plantations where its principal source of food is voles. If barn and tawny owls may be considered to be nocturnal in habit, although barn owl activity seems to peak at dusk and dawn, the short-eared variety is much more diurnal and often to be observed hunting in broad daylight, coursing low over the moors on extremely long wings, in a measured, unhurried flight pattern. Seldom does this bird perch in trees but it frequently uses fence posts as observation sites from which to survey the surrounding vegetation for the slightest sign of vole activity.

A short-eared owl uses a fence post as a vantage point to scan the surrounding area for prey.

Strongly barred plumage on the upper wings and back of brown, buff, black and white, with two prominent carpal patches, gives way to surprisingly light underparts – almost, at first glimpse, white. The facial disc is very prominent with grey markings adjoining the eyes.

The short-eared owl's hunting technique is not unlike that of the barn owl, the quite slow, deliberate wingbeats being followed by a sudden feet-first plunge as prey is located, wings held high as the bird plummets earthwards. An unsuccessful stoop is quickly abandoned, the bird soon resuming its quartering flight.

Short-eared owls are much less sedentary in lifestyle than other species. Indeed, they frequently move territory. This is perhaps best illustrated by the fact that during the recent years of increased conifer plantings, short-eared owls have benefited from these newly created habitats which are rich in small mammal populations. New plantations with their surrounding fences, which are designed to exclude grazing animals such as deer, sheep and cattle, instantly promote a growth in the rodent population, most notably of short-tailed field voles.

However there comes a point in the forest's life when the rapid growth of the trees begins to exclude sunlight and the ground vegetation dies back. It is at this point that the vole habitat goes rapidly into decline and this is often a signal for the owls to move on, perhaps to the next young plantation. Hence it is reasonable to describe the lifestyle of these owls as nomadic.

It follows, too, that short-eared owls are ground nesters. The nest as such is merely a scrape in the ground which is scantily lined with dried grass, sometimes the odd twig and some leaves. In upland areas it is commonly sited in heather, on heatherless hillsides, in tufts of grass and sometimes among bramble patches; in wetland areas the nest is often located in patches of rushes.

Courtship in this species is quite spectacular with the pair soaring together to a considerable height or the cock bird soaring alone above its ground roosting mate. The cock bird also goes through a routine of 'clapping' its wings loudly beneath the body as it flies. There follows a further bonding process which involves soft vocalisation, swaying and bill

A short-eared owl quartering its territory in its search for voles, the main source of food for this particularly long winged owl, typically seen coursing low over marsh, moorland or in young forestry plantations.

A baleful glare from a short-eared owl pictured here in frosted moorland grass. This inhabitant of moors is, unlike most other British owls, a ground nester. However, the nest itself is no more than a collection of strands of grass or heather.

clicking, both of which also feature in the courtship behaviour of tawny and barn owls, and sometimes mutual preening.

As in other owls, the number of eggs laid is very dependent upon the availability of food and can vary from four to fourteen, a high number such as this clearly reflecting a boom year in the vole population. However, vole fecundity is known to fluctuate wildly and sometimes miscalculations occur which may result in the grisly spectacle of the first hatched birds turning on their siblings and consuming them if the parents are unable to catch enough food to sustain the whole brood.

In common with many birds of prey, the interval between the laying of each egg can be a full day, so a brood of short-eared owls can show a huge variation between the first and last hatched. Incubation is between 24 and 28 days, carried out by the female who is fed by her mate. This pattern continues, with the female brooding the youngsters and the male fulfilling the breadwinner's role. The youngsters are flying by the time they are nearly four weeks of age. If voles are particularly abundant, a second brood may follow later in the summer.

Winter populations of short-eared owls in Britain are swollen by migrants from further north, notably from Scandinavia, where conditions become so severe that the only route to survival is to cross the North Sea and spend the winter here. In particularly hard winters, this migration may take some birds into the more temperate climate of Ireland or even further south to the Continent.

From time to time, vole plagues occur and it is then that short-eared owls can sometimes be seen in amazing abundance. There is a delightful Scandinavian fable which suggests that goldcrests, also seeking a more frost-free environment in the winter, sometimes ride upon the backs of short-eared owls as they cross the North Sea. As far as I know, there is no substance to this charming story.

Vocalisation is not a feature of short-eared owl lifestyle. Hissing at intruders and a bit of billing and cooing in courtship are generally all that is heard. However, when intruders do get close to a nest, a cock short-ear will sometimes rise suddenly high in the air, issuing a barking kind of warning yelp.

The tufts on the head, described as 'ears', have nothing to do with the actual ears which, as in all owls, are merely cavities concealed by the head plumage. These tufts are most prominent when the bird is in defensive mode or is alarmed. They seem to have no other discernible purpose.

Long-eared Owl

The long-eared owl, archetype of the 'professorial' owl, is very much a resident of woodland and forest, notably of coniferous forest. Its plumage is more finely and less strikingly marked, especially to the hind part of the wings which thus take on a greyish tinge, when compared with the short-eared or tawny owl, its tail longer and wings shorter than its short-eared counterpart, as might be expected of a woodland dwelling bird. The ear tufts are, as the bird's name implies, longer than those of the short-eared variety. Similarly, they are most prominent when the bird is alarmed or threatened. If there is a belligerence about the expression of a short-eared owl, then the long-eared owl, with its burning orange eyes and almost 'frowning eyebrows', looks positively furious.

This is perhaps the most covert of our owls, shunning proximity with the man-made world and thus seldom seen. Small birds and mammals form the basis of the diet. Long-eared owls are apparently adept at sneaking up on small roosting birds under cover of darkness and literally snatching them from the branches. Sometimes two owls will work in concert when hunting mice and voles, one flushing out the prey, the other pouncing. Presumably the fruits of such combined labours are shared and become a part of the bonding process.

Long-eared owls are largely nocturnal and, because of their colouration, very difficult to spot at their daytime roosts. Habitually, they choose a branch close to the main trunk of a tree, keeping their plumage tight to their bodies if disturbed and thus 'thinning' themselves to become even less obtrusive, ear-tufts raised. Conversely, the long-eared owl can put on an impressive display in defence of its nest, fluffing out its plumage, drooping its

Extremely sedentary in life-style, the long-eared owl favours dense woodland.

wings, raising the ear tufts and giving the impression of greater size.

Although showing a preference for life among the trees, the long-eared owl does break with that tradition on occasion, when it can be seen coursing low over marshland or sand dunes in coastal areas. Indeed, in these circumstances it occasionally nests on the ground, usually under the shelter of a convenient bush. However, much the most favoured habitat is a small stand of conifers surrounded by fields or open country. In such places, they are quite difficult to detect and it seems certain that the long-eared owl is therefore considerably under-recorded in many parts of the country. The current enthusiasm for planting shelter belts might suppose that this will be to the benefit of long-eared owls.

They differ markedly from their short-eared cousins in one other way: far from being nomadic, long-eared owls are particularly sedentary. However, that rule does not apply to Scandinavian long-ears which also decant from their native heath to find winter solace here and further south.

In courtship, there is an interesting variation on the short-eared owl's habit of 'clapping' its wings. In the case of the long-eared owl the 'clapping' is conducted from a perch before the bird launches itself into a display flight.

Following the trait that seems to be inbred in owls, the long-eared owl does not indulge much in nest building, preferring to take over the nest of a crow or pigeon. Five or six eggs are the norm again with incubation largely the responsibility of the female, lasting some 25 to 28 days. The youngsters, like other 'brown' owls, are initially covered in greyish white down and are fed by both parent birds, fledging at about four weeks of age.

In my own experience, I have often only been made aware of the presence of long-eared owls by the noise made by the youngsters when demanding food from their parents. It may best be described as like the sound of a squeaky gate which needs its hinges oiled! Otherwise, long-eared owls hoot. In fact, the hooting may be likened more to a low moan, the sound of which no doubt adds further to the mystery of these elusive birds. During courtship a short, sharp barking note is sometimes uttered and when threatened, a long eared owl, as well as posturing, will hiss menacingly.

When threatened, a long-eared owl can be a daunting sight, fluffing up its plumage to give the impression of much greater size, glaring belligerently and hissing menacingly.

Little Owl

The little owl is really a native of Continental Europe south of the Baltic, which was introduced to southern Britain in the nineteenth century. Favouring farmland, especially where there are extensive areas of hedgerow, this relatively tiny owl gradually spread northwards and positive evidence of breeding in south-east Scotland came to light in the late 1950s. Subsequently, it does not appear to have moved much further north than the Borders region.

This is a very small owl, about the same size as a song thrush, but, of course, identified by its distinctive owl characteristics of a relatively large, blunt head and plump little body.

Being smaller and faster moving than the other owls, the little owl's hunting technique is naturally more direct. It may for instance, break out from its undulating flight to dart into shrubbery or grass as it catches insects, small birds or mammals. On occasions it has been seen to hover momentarily before thrusting its wings up and plummeting onto its prey. It may also be seen attempting to intersept insects in flight.

The bulk of the little owl's diet may consist of insects, but small mammals and birds also find their way onto the diet sheet. When it was first introduced, significantly during the halcyon days of the sporting estates, it was much maligned by gamekeepers and thus frequently persecuted by them, as all owls have been over the years. The persecutors-in-chief accused the little owls of taking vast numbers of partridge and pheasant chicks, a charge later proved to be wholly inaccurate. Close study, in fact, revealed that the little owl consumes large quantities of beetles, earwigs, crane flies and cockchafers, the larvae of which are crop pests.

The most striking feature of the little owl is its yellow eyes which, like those of the short-eared owl, are piercing, also giving this owl an angry expression. It, too, is diurnal in its habits, being most active by daylight, although not exclusively so.

In flight it generally undulates but occasionally it hovers. Most often it is seen perched on a telegraph pole, or on the wires, sometimes on top of hayricks, surveying the ground below for potential prey.

A little owl pictured here in the Lothians, where it reaches the northern limit of its range.

Hardly bigger than a song-thrush, the little owl was once severely persecuted by gamekeepers, accused of taking young game-birds. Careful study however, showed that insects such as crane flies are more popular as prey. This tiny owl is often quite active during daylight hours.

Its most common call is a rather plaintive cooing or muted 'kee-wick' although it does occasionally utter a more whistling phrase. Courtship vocalisation takes the form of a duet, the two pairing birds serenading one another. Offerings of food to the hen by the cock also strengthen the pair bonding. Some posturing at the nest site has been recorded and mutual preening follows copulation.

The little owl shares the collective owl distaste for serious nest building, choosing small tree holes or sometimes holes in the walls of old buildings, occasionally also nesting in burrows but using no nesting material at all. Breeding generally occurs in May when the female broods her clutch of small white eggs – three to five at a time – for some four weeks. Both parents are employed to feed their brood, which take to the wing at about three weeks of age.

The densest British populations still occur in the Midland counties and the south, where they were originally introduced, but there seems to have been some decline in numbers which may be attributed to pesticides and the destruction of hedgerows.

Snowy Owl

The other British owl, if it may be so called, occurs, conversely, in the north of Britain. The snowy owl is really a bird of the polar regions and northern Europe. However, in the late 1960s snowy owls bred in Shetland. In 1967 the well-known naturalist Bobby Tulloch discovered a pair nesting on the island of Fetlar. There had been sightings recorded during the nineteenth century in mainland Scotland, and further recordings were made in the 1950s and 1960s, mostly in the Cairngorms, but this was the first known instance of breeding success, five chicks surviving.

Breeding continued until 1972 when what was presumed to be the same pair, after five years of successful breeding, failed to rear any young. During this period, the male bird attempted to support two females but was unable to maintain an adequate food supply to both, and each year one of the nests was deserted as a result. However, between 1967 and 1975, 22 youngsters were reared, and regular sightings established that they had colonised other islands. Records since confirm sightings in Orkney, St Kilda, Fair Isle, the

Outer Hebrides and the Cairngorms but there is no further evidence of breeding.

Snowy owls feed heavily on small rodent populations. The Fetlar birds were mainly dependent upon rabbits, and the incidence of myxomatosis in the early 1970s undoubtedly contributed to the subsequent failure to breed.

Courtship is always signalled by the male bird's booming voice and his high, circling flight above the nest, which is little more than a depression in the ground with a few bits of vegetation added. The usual posturing follows and sometimes food is brought to the female by the cock bird. Once wooed, she will adopt a begging posture. As in most owls, the pair often indulge in mutual preening once copulation has been completed.

As dwellers in open country, the snowy owl's hunting techniques are less covert than the techniques displayed by woodland owls. Indeed a coursing snowy owl flies in an almost buzzard-like fashion on slow beating wings, sometimes gliding and either suddenly plummeting into the vegetation to catch a small mammal or going into a shallow, accelerating glide to pursue larger prey such as rabbits.

When threatened, for instance at the nest site, a snowy owl can present a fearsome picture, with glaring yellow eyes, wings brought forward and plumage fluffed to apparently increase its size…a sight awesome enough to deter any would-be aggressor.

The snowy owl is a substantial bird, dwarfing other British owls. The cock bird is predominantly white, the female white with grey barring. When seen at close quarters, the yellow eyes are very prominent. It is a ground-nesting bird. Its appearance in Scotland may be due to the fluctuations which occur in its principal prey, lemmings, in Norway or Iceland. In years of shortage, snowy owls are known to 'irrupt' southwards. The origins of the birds seen in Scotland are unknown.

A rare vagrant to northern Scotland, the snowy owl bred regularly on the Shetland Isle of Fetlar during the late 1960s and up until 1975. No further British breeding has since been recorded. It is a native inhabitant of the tundra-like landscapes of Scandinavia.

Owl Facts

BARN OWL

Order:	Strigiformes.
Family:	Tytoninae.
Subfamily:	Tytonina.
Genus:	Tyto.
Latin name:	*Tyto alba*.
Length:	13–14 in (33–36 cm).
Description:	Golden, buff back and wings with discreet grey and white flecking: white face set in heart-shaped facial disc and white under-parts. Dark eyes.
Habitat:	Farmland, stackyards, pasture, meadows, field margins, hedgerows, uncultivated land and rough grazing.
Nesting:	No nest material; lofts, wall holes, church towers, tree holes, occasionally cliffs and old quarries.
Eggs:	Average 4–6, April and May, white, incubated by female, 30–33 days. Nestlings fed by both parents, fly about 9–10 weeks.
Food:	Mice, voles, shrews and rats, small birds, occasionally beetles and frogs.
Some local names:	White Hoolet, Silver Owl, Cailleach-oidhche Gheal (Gaelic) meaning white old woman of the night, Screech Owl, Jenny Howlet, Pudge, Hoolet, Oolet, Gillhowlet, Gil-hooter, Ullat.

TAWNY OWL

Order:	Strigiformes.
Family:	Strigidae.
Subfamily:	Buboninae.
Genus:	Strix.
Latin name:	*Strix aluco*.
Length:	15 in (38 cm).
Description:	Mottled brown, lighter beneath, prominent facial disc, brown and grey phases, dark eyes.
Habitat:	Woodland, hedgerows, town and city parks and gardens.
Nesting:	No nesting material; tree hollows, abandoned squirrel dreys, old crows' nests, old buildings, rock crevices, occasionally on ground.
Eggs:	Lays 3–5 white eggs March to May, incubation by female, 28–30 days. Nestlings fed by both parents, fly about 32–36 days.
Food:	Voles, mice, shrews, young rabbits and rats, small birds, sometimes worms, lizards and beetles.
Some local names:	Brown Owl, Grey Owl, Hoolet, Brown Ullet, Hollering Owl, Screech Owl, Jenny Hoolet, Hill Hooter, Wood Ullat, Wood Owl, Ivy Owl, Beech Owl.

SHORT-EARED OWL

Order:	Strigiformes.	Family:	Strigidae.
Subfamily:	Striginae.	Genus:	Strix.
Latin name:	*Asio flammeus.*	Length:	14–16 in (36–41 cm).

Description: Buff-brown plumage with heavily streaked breast, lighter underneath with two prominent dark carpal patches on wings. Noticeably long wings. Yellow eyes set in prominent facial disc with short ear tufts.

Habitat: Open moorland, young conifer plantations, occasionally marshes.

Nesting: Scrape in ground, often sheltered by heather, grassy tussocks or reed clumps, Little nesting material.

Eggs: April, 4–8 eggs, white and spherical. Incubation by female, 26–28 days. Chicks fed by female (food brought by male), fly about 26 days.

Food: Mostly voles, some small birds, occasionally insects.

Some local names: Hawk Owl, Mouse Hawk, Brown Yogle, Moor Owl, Marsh Owl, Sea Owl, Cat Owl, Day Owl.

LONG-EARED OWL

Order: Strigiformes.

Family: Strigidae.

Subfamily: Striginae.

Genus: Strix.

Latin name: *Asio otus.*

Length: 14 in (36 cm).

Description: Buff with pale mottling and dark streaks. Orange eyes set in prominent facial disc. Long ear tufts.

Habitat: Woodland with coniferous woods preferred. Often chooses small stands of conifers surrounded by open ground.

Nesting: No nesting material; tree hole or old crow or pigeon nest or squirrel's drey.

Eggs: 4–5 white eggs laid March–April, incubated by female only, 25–28 days, fed by both parents, leave nest after 25 days.

Food: Small mammals, small birds and occasionally cockchafers and beetles.

Some local names: Horned Owl, Hornie Hoolet, Tufted Owl, Cat Owl, Long Horned Ullat.

LITTLE OWL

Order:	Strigiformes.
Family:	Strigidae.
Subfamily:	Buboninae.
Genus:	Athene.
Latin name:	*Athene noctua.*
Length:	8–9 in (20–23 cm).
Description:	Grey-brown, barred and mottled with light underwings, short tail and yellow eyes in less prominent facial disc.
Habitat:	Open countryside and hedgerow, farmland.
Nesting:	No nesting material; tree holes, cracks and crevices in walls, buildings or rocks, occasionally in burrows.
Eggs:	3–5, white, late April, early May, incubation 28 days by female only. Nestlings fed by both parents, fly after 5 weeks.
Food:	Insects, beetles, crane flies, small rodents, birds and lizards.
Some local names:	Little Grey Owl, Dutch Owl, Sparrow Owl, Little Spotted Owl.

SNOWY OWL:

Order:	Strigiformes.
Family:	Strigidae.
Subfamily:	Buboninae.
Genus:	Nyctea.
Latin name:	Nyctea scandiaca
Length:	24 in (61 cm).
Description:	Large white owl with light brown flecks (female grey and white bars), yellow eyes, soaring flight.
Habitat:	Tundra-like plateaux or boulder-strewn hillsides.
Nesting:	Ground nester, scrape in the ground with a few strands of lining material such as grass, feathers etc.
Eggs:	White, 3–7, May, incubated by female. Incubation 32–35 days. Young fly at about 45 days.
Food:	Lemmings in Arctic habitats. In Britain where it is now mostly a winter visitor, voles, mice, rabbits and birds up to the size of ptarmigan.

Some local names: Caty Ogle, Jugla (both Shetland).